Cosmic Butterflies
Brief Accounts of Spiritual Realisation

Chapter I

Do not fear for it ha   l love. It is our life and we i accept it as a part of life.
Transformation of the Planet. Good Luck.

This book is dedicated to all of our mankind first and foremost, and this work is thanks to The Living & Moving Trees and Trees of Light, but mostly dedicated to the lessons that life and nature is teaching us. All is in harmony. Even the fundament by which life develops is unique and harmonious. Totality is the fundament not described as an end result however a means in which a time period is manifested through.

Life and nature works and maintains harmony. Good harmony, and fun harmony. If an individual fully understands the nature of love and unity everything becomes a bliss and state. Relationships are all beautiful. Spiritual, individual, objective, according to wilderness. Wild life. A fundamental one must all understand that it is. And always will be. Wild life must be strong, healthy and wise. Our kind is shown everything the way a lot of thought and dedication towards making fruit was put towards. First instances of multiplication. As long as this remains strong respect must be due. There are ways which often mislead our way of thinking. I personally think of this as a movement. It is something which is intrinsic and pure and always good. Fundamentals of understanding it is that wildlife is and it is only concerned with being along the same wildlife. You are different from an animal. You are a wild life form. An organised wild life form. Concerned, I think of

1

stagnant nature, freedom, peace and unity. Sex, love, and all within must come from a place where human nature isn't an accident and that nature and the search for an understanding of a beautiful and fulfilling world is something that I find of value to myself. I must remember the nature of time and the way in which balance is described. Action. The nature of God in your individual world. Iconography in mythologies like that of the centaur and faun, and many others which do not depict present states of nature and the shapes are tied to many wonderful realisations. Albeit still, some moments were and some moments were not. Beautiful is the one who is. For all. It was planned and through a vow. A vow of wildlife. There are plants which understand psychedelia and their nature is to care and it is this fundament that permeates friendship, love, and personal things such as fitness and sex. Always treat knowledge for your kind only. None other. These ideas stem from something conscious and were and will be a key part of the existence of people throughout all of human history. A personal fact. The nature of existence is long and beautiful, although my reality has come to succumb from a permeable lack of love of perseverance and understanding. The apt understanding of time is more than just gibberish nonsense. You must wake up and be not humble. You are there to create and be a part of life. We must not be confined to ideas. The ultimatum of understanding the structured approach is the sense and logic of all things and even life. Life itself is fundamental. Wild.

Plants are individual and all call themselves by different names, some seem to like to feel and some see. Tied to the objective whole of the organism that human beings are, it is important to note how life truly is. Existence does not begin in exclusion of organisms. Therefore the totality of language and understanding cannot be measured by the sum of its words nor by time. I believe in pure essence it is the manifestation of harmonics through flowing water. A butterfly which comes out through all with a whole subject of wilderness. It is full of potential. And a dream of objective. Always listen to what your heart tells you and love everyone equally. But love your woman the most.

Every mathematics of nature pertains to a whole of nature; it is ever changing and some elements are created by the Tree of Light. They do not exist in a true sense. The world and human idea is that of freedom and totality of first and foremost personality, and natures vow, which is something everyone must uphold for their own and for others. It is something which is divine.

The forms of faun, centaur and all other mythological creatures are a fundament created through the force of nature which given the objective of knowledge to many is unexplained. These plants are truly psychedelic. All plants should be. When I want to nourish, I will eat or sleep. It does mean I'm enjoying it. I understand the sense of human dreams. Life. Sex. Responsibility.

First of all, defining the way in which one feels joy is a fundamental flaw of the world. Omnipotence is a key fundament of everything. The world is heading to a very dark place, because it nurtures an idea of objective life and excludes experience and fundamentals of building intellect. Every man and woman go through life. Joy is not what this is. It is either something one must actively fix as a human or something which is a flaw.

Enlightenment is a word with many intricacies and is a perfect time which is A. Defined by love B. Defined by the self and C. Defined by nature of human essence. It is a state of mind which has an all encompassing transcendent mean and utmost personal value. The process of psychedelia permeates time and therefore can be manifested by all things through the intention of the individual. Therefore all of nature must remain whole. And did with perfect sense and logic as I am.

When I began upon collecting my thought and vision I had initially started with an outlook which was of perfection and a symphony of sorts. The core hypothesis of these remains the same however the data analysis became focused on the derivative of man and woman, the nature of pure life, perfect life. The reality of individuality. The state which life is in. It is not a catastrophe that life is. The magnificence of it all is the nature of truth. As one was first born, with sense. The world always looks different. Phases and seasons of life are how you become with the nature of adversity. Everything takes time to realise the most fundamental part, one's memory and creation once realising so is a perfect state for me, and I wouldn't wish anything else for my woman. This highlighted that life is free in all aspects and in existence and freedom is akin to the totality of one circle when it is resolved. The tree is omnipotent, you are, but remember your wildlife and I urge you to think in a sense evolving in a total sense of totality that you may not yet perceive consciously. Each counterpart exchanges from a newly formed union of individual one and upon resolution pertains an aspect of the whole. It highlighted the consequences which life bears upon everything by the very foundation of being free. Natural principles, being the states which define what is needed to feel free. Some individuals don't like incoherence. As a consequence, the divine sense of ancient cultures will defecate. The church exists so it is a state of mind. A meaning of sorts. Time and space. A wildlife is omnipotent to realise confusion but I believe sense is the perfect way to realise. Spontaneity is your life also. But will and wisdom is something I value purely for my everlasting nature, not spontaneity.

The ambiguity of definition of one by individuation given to a being upon embracing the journey of life is not uniform. All environments bear seasons, even the whole system of nature bears seasons, and nature remains fruitful and whole.

The process of transforming the consciousness in a different environment completely is the process of the transformation of the soul. In an essential definition of life, a flower head is a display of crystal characteristics. This does not declassify life but allows for imagination to manifest an idea which is a permeable nature of all of space. Beauty. The Flower of Life. A flower always grows out of one individual stem. The heart is the form within the vesica pisces. And it is the epicentre. The place where one decides upon his body.

Beauty is a trait desired by everybody and therefore it is something which remains pure within the energy force throughout. It ends in a natural state and its perfect impact is something which is often confused with the big bang theory.

The vow of nature is to be perfect and responsible.

Man and woman both are perfect. Then they are not. Then they become again but in a less perfect state. Because in a sense the aptness in beauty is innate; individual and shared between both. It is something which is held within the forms element and it remains until it does.

The parable of Eden makes little for both of us if it is to be taken as a satirical force of pure will and desire which is not boundless. Although from a human aspect this is self defined in all dimensions of understanding, the energy which fruits through your divine character bears similar precepts of bondage when it is something which discards separate nature. Or natura. The THIRD ONLY THING TO BE GRASPED WHOLE AND THE ONLY TO BE GRASPED WHICH CONSTITUTES LAW. ETERNITY IS PART OF THIS LAW.

One's fascination is the whole. To grasp the whole is a process which is bound and therefore be fulfilled. Joy should always be maintained. And joy is pure when laughter is. Intelligence is a fascination. Love is a passion.

One then begins to grasp at something new, from an intellectual standpoint, as this is his nature. This process is a transcendental experience. It is a total reformation of one's idea and fundamental at the core of the individually defined self. IT IS THE SECOND ONLY THING WHICH IS GRASPED. Once a realisation of birth and death occurs, love becomes full. Nothing else is important. Loumin is only love in its purest form as it begins with the letter L.

When clear things of nature are understood without imposing separation a decision is made at every level of the being by the being. These decisions are something which take time or no time.

They take time nonetheless. It is not something that is free of time. Process is what time is. Time is one dimensional and it means it can be perceived, enveloped and transformed by every process and at all times. This earth's time is therapy. Mathematical polarity implies time as one dimensional. A dimension is a whole state present in both aspects of definition.

Children of nature and only of nature. The aspect of union between birth, rebirth, and death. Time is something every individual is granted and it is something that is up to the individual and loved one to take into their own inspiration.

As time is one dimensional, life has one fundamental process. The processes involved encompass the new and the old, but not that which is out of time.

A perfect thing will not come out of time. It is no less perfect.

Chapter II - Action

Individual bio technology and sex were misunderstood and are connected to the process of birth. This is from the simple stupidity principle of evolution. Make use of the world as tools. Find a leaf, tie to a stick. Simple. If you want some herb for later, put it in the tool and use it.

Responsibility. A vow of perfection to nature. Are all essences that are understood by perfection. Whether it be through the willingness to understand its responsibility to not be out of time. Perfection is a harmonious substance equal in both being. All is the same apart from birth.

Intelligence is not individual experience. It is doing what is and operating within law naturally.

Sex is only perfect in a union with one individual, yours truly.

A wonderfully posed explanation of why the earth has overcome an obsessive and compulsive attitude. Perfection is bound by natural principles which are untraceable to other life at most fundamental points of interaction. Whether these fundamentals are of a meaningful and a reasonable interaction and are perfect is another thing. Man had a greater role to play and thus is the great secret. It isn't a separate attitude.

A timely vow to life. A vow to oneself to not be of pursuit is an inharmonic use. It is full and coherent but the nature of the fundamentals of harmony are of a new definition when core pitch, in this aspect idea, is discovered. Sing Lalala, for once. The principle of inharmony is a quality and process and it restructures fundamentals. A way in which harmony is perfect it restructures itself to be in time. A fundamental principle of correspondence and vibration. It is the definition of our dimensional being. One can only imagine what The Tree of Light vowed awards its inspiration.

A salty exaltation! The bliss of nature? Core fundamentals of perfect order? What more!?

From the perspective of creation time surrounded by beings of different nature and equal of own pursuit are deemed lesser when surrounded with. Only being with being whether for pure enjoyment or love or both in a harmonious sense is fully joyfull.

As life is a harmonious experience and requires all tones to be in time for an experience worthy to be called such, a single instance of a full life contains six stages… the cause, the birth, the life, the rest, and the metempsychosis and in some cases the song The Strip Club. I am joking of course. A good thing has happened to me indeed. A perfect quality. Transcendence. For a quality to manifest, not to take away its causal form, it must accommodate inviting harmony. Like anything meaningful in life, it has to be invited towards perception.

Language is the same in application and only different in perception.

Blissful expressions of shape, imposition, and taste of fruit. Come forth. Dews and rainbow of honeyfruit unleash within me. Eden and the all intrinsic and permeable parables come forth in all truth. The scolded free flowing form with a gift pure as the sweetest water. A vow no more perfect than the episteme of delusion. Oh thy wonder is within me and no core of tarnish shall reach me. How perfect is the freedom of balance and way of which nature strides in the vow.

A parable defined by understanding of a phasus which is the law of balance within nature, is what I understood in the whole play. Everything at union and symbiosis. En emanation of the will to be understood as the whole structure of life: void; an all encompassing of the great moral work.

Perfection has a sense of which its appreciation has great value if true and sustained. Not an appreciation that becomes out of time. It is the true nature of awe and gratitude.

Quality has all the meaning of time. To observe time in balance is an action. The incise of action is what is perfect.

Perfection in the states of life should be present at all phases of experience. Light is present at the two states, at the cause and at the moment of metempsychosis. A circle is the only form which is perfect as it defines itself no further than its rejoice and beginning meet. It is the rejoice which means the beginning which forms the whole. Is there a simple sense of wildness?

For a perfect thing to manifest, the being must invite perfection.

The circle can be called a pure perfect form and is a way to represent the idiom of the sacred geometry processes the body undergoes throughout life. The true nature of fulfilment is perfection. Fulfilment is the realisation of the epicentre. That is when perfection is and the circle is not realised until its epicentre. It then begins to cross itself at its sidereal axis and then identifies every magnitude at the tropics and realises at the self. The epicentre.

This state within the soul is not lost for there to be the need for genetics. Its geometrical form is the epicentre realised first. Ah bliss of the egg born which comforts me in a period with every inch of its rich disc.

Every characteristic form defines its own dimension.

The nature of pure and Light intent is what is of the most important faculty of this and individual phenomenon.
Like every work of thought which is diligent, a development will occur in the argument be it from side a or b. This is not without subject to intent. Ideograms are something which at first glance show a structural order and by constantly using the nodes of structural order it is imperative to note that I feel. Nevertheless the nature of life shows sense. Wild nature and free nature constitute symbiotic principles. Competition is not what constitutes symbiosis although some would argue that it is the natural concurrence of decision. This decision lacks the action of individual inspiration of pure ideals.

All things are entities and are separate. We are an organism. They are individual entities. If a place looks truly beautiful it is because it is. Beauty in the natural world is objective. The great plan is still within and life will be in the mechanisms and environments less understood to me. Even wildness. It is a fundamental flaw to not see yourself as an individual amongst many and a part of the organism. Human action poses the question to true wildlife in all forms 'why?'. And it is important to realise the role of freedom and the divine blueprint for all things included in nature and not to confuse them with your organism. Bees are a form of beauty at the highest potential. Love for children which is often difficult but it is a mechanism which will remain whole. Bees are linked to knowledge and psychedelia in general. From an evolutionary perspective they are bears. They have their own vow and are what formed through wild animals in the void structures and throughout all their known systems of logic. It is what makes them a part of nature and it is why they remain and will always be a part of said nature. They understand their life fully and their form is not subject to evolution but rather a spirit which is encompassed within their nature. They are birds at will because they want to do so, they are insects because they also do. The phenomenon of the exchange of the ant carrying a tree branch is something that is still seen in nature today as a symbol more intricately connected to the grand ritual of the whole. Their DNA does not go through a change. They possess the same but a less defined quality of life. The seed is something that does not appear in pre designated locations. This ritual is seen as the making of the natural vow by the whole colony. All of nature is in conversation. The nature of our organism is something intrinsic with their system as it is independent and its reflection is in our organism the same way. A way of respect.

The faults of certain nature are fundamental, because to bear gifts upon everything around you is material. Sight of how the world is and as God a state of union and harmony one must realise the respective objective of it all. Nudity is fundamental. Intellectualising nudity is wrong.

May I say that I have run forth and across the foot of the celestial ocean in a place misunderstood from the point of view of birth. From the start of my life, my goal was to attain knowledge. Knowledge of the highest order. As a little child I would read "Egypt", a monthly magazine about the ancient culture that lived there. I remember being fascinated by what the magazine was writing about, but my favourite topics were those which focused on religious life and ritual. Its religion developed to be characterised by wilderness or death. Realising the preservation of life is a constituent of a realised individual. Everything pertains to the law of life and it is nothing to fear.

I was raised a Christian by my grandmother. When I moved from Poland to the UK, aged 12, I cut ties with Christianity. Although I was not an atheist, I would not call myself agnostic. Somewhere within me, I knew the answer wasn't as simple as the existence of God. I believed in life after death and the immortality of the soul, and today, I do not believe, but rather know these things to be true. A realised being is a being and cannot be defined, only through the self.

As I matured, I started to explore Buddhism and meditation. At age 20, I joined the Rosicrucian order and started exploring the occult sciences despite reservations from my family. Although I couldn't afford to pay the dues for membership and spent a very long time with the Order, I cherish every meditation and everything I have learnt. At around the age of 23, my life started to change. I became obsessed with philosophy and esoteric knowledge, and made it my goal to read the works of all the ancient philosophies and study mythological precepts to a great detail. Around that time, my Third Eye opened and my life changed forever.

At this point in time, to bear a child is a fundamental process of birth and rebirth of everything. This statement is a fundamental flaw of it all. The organism is everything, it is key to understand.

I feel that with the new age of technology we are all responsible for contributing to one another in a positive and meaningful way. There has never been a more adequate time to explore spirituality. The challenges our world faces generate a need for spiritual development. Wars, economics and consumerism have all contributed to the 'degeneration' of our individual existence. We are no longer carefree. Our overlords have managed to domesticate our wild anima. The spirit is kept in a cage where money and meaningless responsibilities are the steel bars. Most of us need help. The way our lives are led to depression and various psychological disorders. Through festivals of living soul organisms they are things that end up disrupting the world within and reflect in a quantum way in the way the soul works. THE way the soul is, must remain clean. It is something not to be taken lightly, as it is beauty and part of the gift.

Throughout my early life on this planet, I have struggled to remember key things about my life and felt lost - let's use the word 'ambient'. A few years ago, I had a pretty unwilling experience, however, this turned my life around. I had experienced many things after this 'breakdown' of ego, that I can only attribute to the divine aspect of life and equally myself.

I began to eagerly study philosophy and mythology to try and grasp an understanding of the objective. Philosophy presented me with many normal but also quite trivial questions. I was expecting to find answers regarding life, reality and nature - not points regarding common sense ethics shrouded by figures pertaining to immoral and sin of the only and greatest kind. Although in today's world we cannot fully grasp a sometimes 4000 year gap in language or perception, I was surprised.

After my breakdown, my life changed forever. I started to have profound psychosomatic experiences, visions and revelations. It was as if my yearning for higher knowledge had been answered by something. Now, my biggest question: what was this 'thing' that had heard my call. Was I speaking with God? An angel? After years of chaotic beliefs in polytheism (which still applies to the knowledge I subsequently gained) I found my answer.

I suppose the main chunk of this book will be dedicated to the expression of this divine force. My knowledge comes from within and from visions and conversations with these divine forces. With this handbook, I aim to share my first hand experiences from my spiritual journey and divine knowledge withheld to me by the Tree of Life. To me, these experiences are profound. Despite many hours that I dedicated to research, I could only find a small number of things that were relatable to my experiences. I still have many questions, and fortunately my age is on my side. As a 28 year old, I have a whole life of contemplation and development ahead of me.

A big part of me is in discontent with how the world operates. Most of us are stuck with careers that leave us unfulfilled and lives which don't reflect in any way the wild natures that we are at our core. The process of our domestication starts with fear. They say fear is your worst enemy, and they are right. We fear what the loss of our job would mean, we fear war, we even fear what a close friend would think of us if we told them a secret. Why? Our ego manifests a barrier between us and others. This is known to psychologists as individuation. Yes, it is necessary and good to uphold individuality in the world, however this must be done in a healthy way.

From a youngsters perspective, the influence of social media and entertainment on trends which we are subject to, makes room for an unhealthy 'rat race' and sometimes even 'war' between people. Is a car worth in excess of a million euros really necessary and will it make us happier and project the feeling of being fulfilled? In all real life applications, no. Individuals who seek material assets with the goal of fulfilment have succumbed to the consumerism and indoctrination of today. In today's age it is key to remember our currently fragile human nature and try to strengthen our spirits in a holistic and full way.

All of us have an obligation to contribute to our communities and relationships in a wonderful way. We must dedicate time to heal ourselves and to help and heal others. We are desensitised and this is what makes us so fragile. In no way did I imagine a world where I am dehumanised by my surroundings. I see this in music, art, literature and by the way people behave. The main reason I am writing this book is to help people understand the beautiful substrate of our being, which, I hope, will lead them to a great place of transcendence. I hope my words will lead to an inspiration for many of you.

The information held in this body of work comes from personal revelations, dreams, visions, my contemplation of nature and a study of symbolism in ancient Greek religion and mythology as well as my studies with the Kabbalistic method.

Some of the information in this book may be seen as absurd to those who are just beginning their journey of spiritual and self development. Those who have seen past propaganda and our societal structure and stigma may find a refreshing world view set out in this volume.

I have experienced things in my life which at a less mature stage I attributed to the work of a higher power or 'God'. At this point in my life, I believe the truth which is God - only in nature and consciousness. My view of personality and form is archetypal. We are all different and new archetypes are constantly being forged by the universe.

I hope you will find some valuable information in this book. I urge you to keep an open mind and to humble any pre convictions. The past 7 years of my experiences will be put forward here alongside some thoughts on how to find your own light of wisdom.

Through my humble enlightenment I have realised that I am an old spirit who has gone through many cycles of spiritual evolution. I haven't been alive for a very long time, yet I have managed to shed the veil of death and time and remember what is most important to me, all thanks to the divine Tree of Light. My mission here is to help younger beings understand the objective and develop spiritually. I must stress that it saddens me. I must scream through the silent work to raise an alarm on the life form I have experienced.

With the aid of technology I am glad to present a short handbook of philosophical and spiritual concepts which I hope will inspire you to do further research yourself. My personal experiences are presented here to show what mankind is capable of achieving with the right mindset.

Chapter One: The Human Void

The Environment

Geography, every principate of phi is life bearing. Our omnipotence is more objective and essentially void of polygamous relation. It is life bearing and awe inspiring.

The Flower of Life & The Mechanisms of Creation

The universe was always a great mystery for me. How did I come to life, was one of the many questions which came into my existence. I couldn't have just appeared.

In the ancient mystery schools we see a symbol known as the Flower of Life. It is a master key to understanding the mechanisms of what is responsible for our lives. It is a contemplation of what we call God as well as aspects of human nature. It is an ideogram as well as a geometric gate which allows us to understand how everything came to be. The fascination with the gift of life is nothing wrong.

One must accept that the universe was once baron and nothing lived. Through proportion, the Flower of Life depicts all known phenomena that occur throughout all of space. It describes the formula for light, sound, states of matter, life force, reincarnation and all known living biomes and species. It is a mean of sorts.

All conceptualised matter and forms are particles and minerals in what quantum physicists call the 'fabric of space'. They are not within objective space themselves but rather beyond. This is sometimes called 'the void'. This void also had an origin and it was most likely a series of feedback processes where objective space took various forms. Water, gases, liquid of other nature and of course minerals. I believe minerals which generated energy within the objective space were some of the first structures to appear, although I believe water to be one of the primordial matters which manifested. The wisdom of life should not be seen as a mere accident of unfortunate events. Beautiful mathematics shall always be preserved equal.

Within water, primordial molecules formed as it is conductive, which energised the substance and forced particles contained in the void to quantum leap and attach to the energy permeating the water. This was the birth of consciousness within all life forms. For all. The seed is something that should be maintained eternally.

The energy congealed the water and formed clusters which manifested new quantum particles within the void and forced the phenomenon of sonoluminescence within the objective space and then within the void. This reflected itself within the 'jelly'. This was the birth of light and the foundations of the mathematics of the human eye. It is also the birth of the All Seeing Eye which is known to us as the Tree of Light (commonly known as The Tree of Life).

The sonoluminescence which occurred in the void allowed the energy which permeated the water to leap into the 'bubble' caused by the sonoluminescence which occurred within the void. This 'fermented' the void so to speak and due to this a particle of boundary was formed and divided mineral systems held within the makeup of the void.

This process was already something which was predefined by the characteristic force of energy. Not something which occurred through a violent dominance caused by an atomic charge or discharge.

The void is somewhat of a never ending atomic clock. One should familiarise themselves with the concept of spontaneous generation - it is as simple as the number 1 in a more literal sense.

Life is not made up of the same resonant frequency as the physical world. They are completely separate entities. Life has the attribute of assimilation and is adaptive, therefore it can appear in the physical world and withstand the atomic charge of non living matter. It is a system whose primary order is energy and form.

You have 2 halves which are a separate entity, the force of life and the void. The number 0 is the first number and ideogram that is representative of two parts which make up the objective reality or world. These are the physical world which constitutes matter and the mechanics of balance which allow both energies to exist in harmony.

The void is something which existed prior to objective space but all are a collected sum. The void and objective space are physical matter and the void has an effect on objective space through the motion and energy of the atomic clock. The atomic clock is the third structure which exists in the universe. This formed numerous condensations in the objective space which became solid due to low temperatures and had radioactive properties. This is the reflection of the atomic clock which is the core mechanism of physics themselves.

If we take the process described earlier and apply it to the principles of this mechanic we see that it is a physical process of creation which enables life force and physical force to achieve balance.

I believe the concept of the trinity to be that which describes life in the best way. So far we have discussed the concept of physical and non living forms as well as a characteristic of life as well as the principle quality of the energy of the structure of balance.

The structure of balance is still and does not change. It is reflected in a law of polarity and causality best described in the hermetic principles.

In the physical idiom, we have the nature of atomic charge of positive, neutral and negative. In the idiom of life it is the characteristic of spontaneous generations.

Spontaneous generation is an intrinsic quality of both the physical world and life, however reflected in different aspects of their character. In the physical world, this is manifested as the way particles maintain structure, and in life this structure manifests in the manner of it appearing. It is an intrinsic and definite quality of life rather than a structural quality, although it is both. The physical world emanates everything that life is. Both structures exist simultaneously and one is not the result of the other. People believe this because of the misunderstanding of sonoluminescence being in colour as well as the phenomenon of water.

This is reflected in the very nature of the physical world we live in, which itself is a union of all the orders of form. This is where an important division occurs in an idiomatic sense.

I am a person who believes in the principle of cause and I would go as far as to say I know it is true. As I am the effect of the cause, a principle of it and its part I can perceive it however I cannot structure how the physical organism came to being. Because you are a seed which occurs in water. You metamorfosize into with sonoluminescent brilliance, not organised wild life, which doesn't make sense.

To elaborate I believe in the existence of the Tree of Life (I call it the Tree of Light). I had visions which showed me how it looked and will describe some of those experiences later on. Not only did I see the tree, but also visions of the very first life forms. The universe is a lot more fantastic than it first appears to be. The period of cosmogony was the first period of life which the Tree brought forth. I have memories of this and visions form the basis for my knowledge. This is not a hypothesis.

The whole and pure nature of life which is embodied already exists in the form of the monad, or The Tree of Life. Humans are the fruit of it. We are an embodiment of the pure life however our nature is the pure life with the union of the physical world manifested in our characteristic form. The Tree of Light also possesses sight and hearing and life giving properties. It produces us. We are very advanced stick insects fundamentally. I reserve a little bit of humour when I make this statement. I will give further evidence for this in a later chapter when discussing my personal spiritual experience.

The Human Void

The natural world is full of meaning. Its realm holds many lessons for the observer. Understanding symbols that lay in the natural world can lead to many revelations and open doors to a higher understanding of one's own being: spiritual, psychological and physical.

I make the distinction between spirituality and psychology on purpose, although they are connected. Many of us have spiritual goals, theories and motivations - be it meditation or prayer. Despite psychology being a mechanism of the self, I see it as a separate entity from spiritual practice. As there is 'one' objective truth - spirituality can be assumed as a monism. Psychology on the other hand has a primary division of male and female - instinct and intuition - and then a further divisive force: its constant shaping by the self and the environment throughout our lives. This shaping force could be interpreted as the monad.

It is an intricate system of relativity and all the principles and laws which constitute the world are a reflection and inflection of one another. They are all which form the number 0.

People who have asked questions about their own nature often ask what is the driving force behind our psyche. It is simply our conscious energy - not the ego. The same goes for the physical - in human terms, the simple definition is that of male and female.

Primarily, the ego is a combination of libido, self awareness and motivation which is not of sexual nature. We see a conjunction of forces that are spiritual, psychological and physical. One may fall in love, seek a deeper understanding of self or be motivated to create art or music. All these actions are interconnected and although their occurrence may not have internal factors, they are all a part of what makes us individual.

This is the reflection of the eternal law of energy and magnetism. It is one which exists and a second which exists with it.

The ego itself is not what I call a 'soft' phenomenon - something which is observed but its origin has no physical grounding. The brain is capable of generating millions of chemical variations. It is in brain chemistry where we find the object of the ego. To my understanding, the brain produces a chemical which stores information about how we react to a given perceptible (music, aesthetic, colour, people). Its makeup and functioning is shaped by our waking state as well as our dreams. The natural balance of the chemical is translated into hormones which then make for attraction between man and woman.

The phenomenon described as 'ego death' is the breakdown and reconstruction of this chemical structure. Through experiencing a 'shock' of sorts or discovering profound information, the psychological structure of our reason begins to transform. A new set of impulses is generated and this new group replaces the old one.

The process of 'ego death' is a transcendental state where the laws of creation manifest within the chemical structure of mind and can be interpreted as spiritual experience. It can have positive and negative effects. We see the reflection of the monad within our subtle bodies.

I believe that to fully understand where we are now as people, we must undertake the journey of exploring the birth of space, prehistory of life, the various natural systems and finally our own culture. Studying these topics is beneficial for those that seek answers. The knowledge gained can lead to rich and fulfilling individual thinking and ultimately a better feeling within one's self.

With the utmost humility, I must express that I have been lucky enough to experience my own archetypal force to the fullest extent possible at this current time, and albeit my humble enlightenment is of individual nature, some may find interest in what I write here.

The search for meaning is a fundamental process of every sentient human. Whether it is something small or grandiose, every one of us has questions about the nature of the world we live in. This inquisition of sorts, is a very beautiful thing and I encourage everyone to not see the lack of answers as anything negative. The process itself is something that holds a comforting force and its ethos is that of higher consciousness.

This existentialism that arises takes its source from not knowing fundamental truths about existence and the fear of there only being one instance of consciousness that a given individual can experience. I believe that our natural curiosity succumbs when no breakthroughs, conscious or not, are achieved. These breakthroughs often happen in deep sleep, where a tranquil veil is placed upon our soul and everything becomes familiar and known.

I am lucky enough to have remembered my previous incarnations at a relatively mature but young age. These memories have laid to rest any existentialist dissatisfactions and have allowed me to meditate upon the deeper questions regarding my individual existence. Whether one can remember or not, please rest assured that our soul has the potential to be infinite, however one must not forget that the responsibility of reaching 'immortality' lies within.

For those who fear, do not, as this attainment can be very simple as the conditions for it are set out individually and not as a collective. One may simply be at the gates of 'blissful unawareness' and still experience emotions and thoughts that accommodate for infinite reincarnation. Keys to this state are love, happiness and peace of mind.

The role of karma is fundamental. Our karma is the energy connected to our conscious experience and action. If one is true to individual valour and principle at all times, there is no need to worry about karma impacting them negatively. Although transpersonal, I have found that karma is something very important for the existence of the individual and is a key principle in achieving immortality. One must be fair to one's own self and to the self of others.

States of enlightenment are even more impactful upon the karmic balance. If one has reached a place where the secrets of existence have unfolded, I would urge not to waste time and to develop to one's limit, as there are possibilities of transcending this state to future incarnations. Upon reaching my enlightenment I have made this my goal.

It is possible to maintain awareness at the moment of death. This is something which has caused inspiration for my study. To not lose memory and to continue to experience our divine human nature is something I wish to accomplish one day.

One can look at the nature of consciousness like a fire. With a controlled input of good quality kindling, the fire is well shaped and eternal, whereas with too much kindling it spreads into chaos.

Being, Non-being, Minerals & Energy, Purpose

Knowledge is acquired, possessed and sometimes shared by the substance which holds it.

Since the birth of intelligence life has been seeking the answer of the origin of all things and being. Many struggle with the notion of there being nothing before 'it all' happened. I, myself, found it very difficult to accept. There is no doubt that the mental and real world have many energetic processes responsible for the formation of matter or transfer of information, as well as structures relating to the formation of celestial bodies and the systems they are a part of.

Humanists have pondered upon the question of 'being and non-being' in the aspect of life and death. The same discussion applies when thinking about the formation of the void. It is worth pointing out that I write from the perspective of the universe being an ever changing structure, which in itself had to evolve and develop to where it is now. It expanded, collapsed, regenerated and so on. In energetic principles it is most likely a series of feedback and static processes. This leads me to a categorization of energies into generative, informative and measurement forces.

The magnificence to grasp the subtle mechanics of a single metaphysical plant is simply enough to say, to not want to comprehend everything, is, ignorant. I must stress the universe's beauty through this volume.

These different types of energies exist in their own systems which occur in the physical realm. The generative process arises from tension within a group of minerals, the informative has its own combination of minerals and so does the measurement force. To develop further, I will categorise the minerals as those which are elemental, structural and formative. Within those mineral clusters, various elemental processes arise based on atomic tension.

The ancient South American civilizations (and not only) understood that harmonics were reflections of elemental forms. Their study of cosmogenesis was based on the elements and the structures which those elements arose from. They understood that these element generating structures were grouped and that some created impulses. They saw natural diversity as an underlying law and logic which permeated all aspects of existence.

Now, what gives birth to those minerals in the first place? The universe fundamentally had a simpler structure and mechanic at its beginning. Its initial 'purpose' or 'goal' was to uphold its own form and define the laws of its independent constituents. What gave birth to this initial structure? The ancient schools developed a theory of spontaneous generation, which stated that a living organism could arise from nonliving matter.

We could apply this concept to the study of physics and yield interesting conclusions when drawing parallels between our own workings as human beings and the systems in non living matter. Accepting the theory of spontaneous generation with regards to physics, would lead to a satisfying conclusion of the phenomenon of 'free will' and undermine the deterministic viewpoint of human logic, assuming that the physics of the void is a function and that this function is concealed within human consciousness. I believe all human mistakes translate through a pure and imminent soul of essence which is held within every form of organism. It is important to learn and envision a world without such mistakes. The nature of this is extremely subtle, as is our thought process and behavioural pattern which arises from a depression. This depression does not have to have a negative connotation, it can be a blissful expression of purity and joy and yet cause a perplexion in later life which is a natural state of balance.

In my contemplation, 'free will' can be attributed to a spontaneously generated quanta particle which is independent in action, and attaches itself to a specific frequency in the resonant matter of space. This particle 'chooses' when, and which frequency to attach itself to and its behaviours are the building blocks of the process of free will, humour and libido in living organisms. The switch may potentially happen at a very large timescale and as a result of this process new things are generated in the cosmos, a new archetypal energy, mineral or resonant field.

The resonant matter responsible for the upholding of the void has its own function and property. These frequencies form fields which allow the cosmos to make decisions about what matter does. Every chemical in the universe has an index of information which it carries within itself. As an example we see that chemical bonding is a controlled process where a+b can only result in being ab. Another more direct example is the transmutation of matter from solid, liquid and then gas. This example can expose there being a principle of index within a given material structure.

Through the law of correspondence it is said that all things are resonant with one another. This resonant field must be balanced and in harmony for the structure of the world to be upheld. I must stress this expression is valid in all aspects of our existence. It is also present throughout the moment of rest and has implications upon the form of our organism. This implication can be very negative upon the Tree of Light.

The forces mentioned above are the primary make up of a fourth force we call consciousness through the principle of correspondence. Matter itself is not void of consciousness, although its nature may be more quantized, its existence makes it apparent. All matter is in a sense hybrid and adaptive. There are not only characteristic changes based on the environment but also structural changes that are based on the condition of the matter in question.

Our organisms hold all the processes that are in the non living foundation. There are photons, so our eyes absorb them, there are vibrations in the air, so we hear sound. The generative process is responsible for inspiration, action and love. We absorb information in the environment and make decisions based on our observations. It is difficult to see a world which simply exists without its own self defining purpose.

In the body, we have mineral holding glands in our organs which are responsible for the correct distribution of energy and functioning of life force.

The Multiverse

Throughout my spiritual journey, I have received numerous visions regarding the space we live in. The nature of the world always fascinated me, and I held fundamental questions at the forefront of my meditations. I wondered about the size of our world, the relative size of our planet to others, and how many worlds there are in total. Before stating what I saw in my visions, I will stress that space is really, and I mean really vast. Its size relative to ours is already large when looking at just our own bubble of the observable universe. If one is to go beyond our universe, and try to quantify the whole, we would be looking at relative infinity.

The grand cosmos, which is the largest structure I managed to observe, operates like a solar system. It is made up of spherical chasms which rotate around a sun-like mineral. Within this we have universe clusters which hold thousands if not millions of universes within them. I observed that there are 5 clusters rotating around this sun-like mineral structure. There are many of these universe groups, not just one.

The grand cosmos is located on a topographic plane which, like the earth's topography, is subject to atmospheric changes which afflict the structural property of the universe which is manifested. This results in the formation of a multitude of life forms and some more obscure pockets of space accommodate for life forms such as dragons.

Each of the smaller universes has its own laws of physics, chemistry and biology. There are a multitude of different life forms in the world. I have been lucky enough to access my individual akashic record. In this experience I remembered my past lives and saw myself in different life forms, not just human. Albeit they can be considered human, they differ fundamentally from one another.

Anima

Here, I will attempt to conceptualise the term anima in the aspect of consciousness and through the process of rest also known as metempsychosis. It is imperative to note that both are interconnected.

In terms of life and death one could not exist without the other. Both consciousness and the state of metempsychosis display the characteristics of one another. Consciousness animates the Tree of Life and vice versa both in the state of rest and in the state of life. I am proposing an argument that vital energy (anima) of the life mechanic, animates the structures of the physical dimension and allows for the organised systems of matter to form. It is imperative to note that the wellbeing of the soul, mainly governed by purity, has a direct effect on the state of the Tree of Light. It is what allows for humanity to distinguish between both individual and objective good.

Now, this anima has many dimensions. We could call gravity a form of vital energy because it promotes order within the celestial systems. On a more direct level, the spontaneous generation of particles would arise from a system of vital energy, forming the building blocks for life and the material world. It is more probable that energy is the source of matter, rather than the opposite.

Spontaneous generation must be a materialisation of a force or a multitude of forces. I believe these particles to be in a way the will of the law of order or balance. They are non the less the mechanisms which are responsible for the inspiration of life.They accumulate a property which allows for the individual expression of matter. We can note that the void has the quality to be animated by energy and our quality as life which is all encompassing also resonates within the energies of creation and cosmogony.

From the example of gravity, we can infer that 'anima' operates on fundamental levels throughout all of existence. It is not only something apparent in living organisms. The universe has laws which operate within their means and those laws are what constitute the principle of anima. It seems that it is a universal principle and that matter is animate in a more peculiar sense, be it via the movement of electrons or otherwise.

For life to exist in the universe, there have to be fundamentals set in stone in the very fabric of every resonance within the energy makeup. This is not in a cold sense, but rather in the aspect of the already living forms. Each constituent of those fundamentals is relative to others forming the whole. It has to be something deeply embedded in the structure of the universe. The void is not only animate within itself but it also possesses something within.

With my spiritual experiences to provide a backdrop for my thinking, I am only pondering upon the existence of the monad, and not myself. There is a greater force at the core of human existence, which gives life, guides and is conscious and has to remain healthy. It is important to remember, and also something to experience in every understanding of the term health. The magic of the world is far greater than anyone could collectively comprehend. It is our time to live after all.

On The Intellectual Process

The intellectual process and the derivative of logic is very complex. It is also a fundamental quality of our lives and also our wellbeing. When shaping our world view, we resonate with ideals or dismiss them because we feel that they are untrue or that they are immoral. This choice itself is an analysis we make.

We can categorise our undertakings in this analysis as being conclusions based on life experience or from a secondary or tertiary source of information. The process of differentiating via direct experience can be called organic reasoning while differentiating via indirect experience can be called inorganic or synthetic reasoning.

The same applies to a collective decision and implication upon one's actions in the sense of communication of all kinds. An all encompassing truth.

I want to bring forward the distinction between two types of synthesis of thought and action which relate to the modes of differentiating via direct experience or secondary sources.

Organic synthesis would be the formation of the subject of awareness where án idea is based on direct experience alongside personal conviction, whereas inorganic synthesis would be the formation of the subject of awareness where the thesis is based on a secondary source.

The subconscious process can be divided into the same categories. A process where direct experience is the foundation and a process where an indirect source is of influence. The former has a much greater impact as personal experience is much more direct as opposed to a pre conviction based on absorbing information. It is after all something that has directly influenced our existence. The subconscious is vital to uphold in a healthy way. It itself is a faculty of reason which often learns through the state of sleep as well as through direct experience.

When we discuss key existential topics such as life after death or the existence of Deity, we may be inclined to relate our reason with the organic principle of our understanding as these points of argument are something most people find individually important. One may feel a strong conviction to argument 'a' without prior study, and this conviction will drive him or her to support that stance.

This support by association is something very interesting, as it sheds light on our inner language which is often silent. This language is deeply rooted in culture and social dynamics. It is the language of intuition which originates in the subconscious mind and comes into light during the dream state. The way we behave is deeply alarming. Our use of physical objects to instil an emotion in people is something pleasing when done with the whole of the being, and not with an already skewed state. There are many things, and in a very direct sense, the invention of money has caused stress upon the relationship between collective subconscious learning and the learning through direct conscious experience. It forms bias within our chemistry and alters the way people appear and perceive the whole as free energy manifests in a place which it shouldn't. These chemicals are often stress related and are severely detrimental to the harmony of energy which is self resonant. The principal quality of this chemistry is dissonance. This language is mostly affected as part of the general characteristic of life energy and it emanates the force of self awareness.

As a result mania can arise. Mania can be viewed as the loss of the faculty of reason. In a positive light it can be a very reflective and indescribable experience, however there is a fundamental shift which occurs at the foundation of our energy harmony if this is translated into a cohesive pattern by our life force. The consequences are individual. The individual has begun to access the language of dreams and because of its complexity cannot fully manifest its meaning in the life he is experiencing. This language is embedded in every one of us, and through collective uprisings of the unconscious force, it manifests as cultural ideology and cultural individuation.

This is the point when the magnificence of life is in full swing and the intricate and the nature of our beings swing in a very free and naked way. Although for me, it has been poetry and not a mass of Mozart I must caution people who begin to feel new emotions in places where they do not feel comfortable. I will simply make the point that buildings are not comfortable. Everything we are surrounded by is not the pure intent of the world. The pure intent of the world is something which we are, but must separate an objective view from.

The ideas of conversation with the Divine are the conception of the ideals held in higher consciousness. When ideas like this are nurtured, the individual begins to operate in a higher dimension of consciousness.

The dimensionality of consciousness can have physical consequences. It is apparent in the way people have come to look. This is apparent in young individuals who begin an interest in political or spiritual matters. This is the beginning of the formation of ideals which are inspired by the collective good and self progress rather than self preservation. This mode of thought can manifest because the internal conviction of the immortality of the soul has been achieved and a goal to achieve this state of spirit has been set. This can occur even when the realisation is of subconscious means. This adaptation is of a positive nature in most cases.

Mania arises from the pathology of the media and information we absorb, stress and many other factors. In today's world, most people have experienced and are touched by mania. As well as psychological it also has physical properties. It is apparent in the way we function. The dying of the hair, piercing of the nostrils, etc. It is a very sad sight to see how we have come to function. Our society has come to glorify pain and suffering through film and even the beautiful arts of music, conversation and painting have succumbed.

Since the industrial revolution the stress of survival has overcome the need for spiritual practice and has become the primary worry of many people today. Without a natural inclination to lead a healthy spiritual practice within one's life there are little to no everyday opportunities to develop spirituality. It puts a great fear into my own life, despite the knowledge bestowed on me. It is something which we must deal with individually while maintaining core principles of serenity.

I had faced this problem when I was young, where a deep and uncomfortable feeling of existential drought would manifest in my gut. Luckily, I was naturally inclined towards spirituality and my greatest wish was to grasp the mechanics of creation and the world.

It is common that the individual starts to identify higher beings, and begins to associate them with everyday occurrences which seem synchronous to his newly developed ideals. This spontaneous correlation is not an abstraction of normality, but rather a state of openness achieved by activating new neurochemicals and pathways.

On The Nature of Language

Language and script is something that has fascinated me for many years. I often pondered where the inspiration for terms came from and what influences did nature bare on the language we speak and write today. I found that writing is deeply rooted in the celestial bodies and natural forces such as the wind and rain. One can simply study the geometry of letters and the structure of words to uncover hidden meaning. Once this process has been analysed the influence of the natural world is apparent.

If we analyse the word 'natura' letter by letter we can come to an understanding of the depth of influence nature and the world has on our thinking and communication.

Let's start with the letter 'N'. When written it is three lines which ascend, descend and ascend again. The geometric quality of this letter indicates that there is something we are standing on and that there is something above, as well as something appearing in the heavens. This would be the Sun. The letter 'A' in contour shows us light which is above, the Sun during the day and the Moon at night. The letter 'T' could indicate light, rain and also trees and generally in this context something which comes from above or something that grows from below. The letter 'U' could indicate water or wind. The letter 'R' can indicate the rain, wind, the cold or the sun setting. 'A' could indicate darkness at the end of the day and the appearance of the Moon in the sky.

When dividing the word into three syllables 'na-tu-ra' we can see that 'na' would be the sunrise from darkness, 'tu' would be the day, as 't' symbolises light and 'u' wind, and 'ra' would symbolise the setting of the sun and a different form of light appearing in the night, this form being the Moon.

In this system of understanding, names seem to be a sort of prayer or blessing given to the individual carrying it. When analysing my name, 'Aleksander', I found it deeply connected to a blessing of the sun and moon, health and longevity.

'A' - may the Sun, that which comes from light
'D' - from above may there come energy, being tall
'A' - strength, protection from breaking bones
'M' - may the Moon and that which is light

We sense that there was something in nature that was omnipresent and that the Sun and Moon were the first anchor, or reference point when perceiving this force.

In animism we see the personification of natural forces such as wind, rain, sunlight and season. This has impacted linguistic psychology and phonetics. Spoken word around the world reflect the natural environment and actions of people. Angular letters like

A,K,S reflect action and process while rounded letters like O,M,U reflect states and quality.

In the journey of self development it is imperative to study one's own body language and the body language of others. The animation of the limbs or the inclination of one's stance or tone of voice is sometimes different from that which is spoken out loud. Some mechanics may become motoric reflexes and be a certain 'mode of default' which the individual enters when dealing with others. This action incurs stress in the vital energy system. It is a sign of mania.

Communication is said to be learnt through imitation. Verbal communication is one thing, however the language of the divine is a universal thing. I often find myself speaking a completely different language when dreaming. I understand what is being spoken to me and can use said language, however when I want to engrave new information into my waking state, I have to manifest symbols within the dream state to conceptualise them.

I believe that humans have a natural language and the language we are using now is something of a parable of the mother tongue, hence the development of religious ideologies. It is perhaps something that is being formed, rather than something which has devolved from our existence, although the current situation in the world leaves me with little hope.

Chapter Two: On God, The Tree of Life & Cosmogony

As my spiritual journey began, I knew that there was a force, spirit or something greater than my individual. Initially, I was intrigued by the idea of polytheism. In Greek thought, humans are said to be the offspring of the Titans.

I found myself speaking to a force which I attributed to God and found these conversations an aid in personal development. Many years passed and I became more inclined towards a holistic approach which was centred around the natural world.

I began studying Green Magic and Paganism. I found a fascination in the symbols of honey, nectar, bees and the hummingbird. I started to perceive an organism which embodied life force and the whole of humanity as one web of being. I started to search for what this organism could be and the answer was simpler than I could imagine.

Despite religion and spirituality being universal, we see diversity around the world which pertains to this subject. Although characteristics like polytheism and animistic personifications of nature are seen throughout the world, they differ from culture to culture. There is one theme however, that is universal and is seen around the world without exception and this is the Tree of Life.

It was the summer of 2022 when I experienced a vision and the most profound revelation of my journey. I saw a miraculous tree which had a luminescent sphere in the centre of its trunk and similar spheres growing around its base, coming out of the roots, some distance from the trunk. These oval shaped spheres emanated light and the Tree could change what colour was coming from the spheres. Red, yellow, blue, white and so on.

I was amazed by its beauty. I saw this Tree in a very lucid dream and woke up straight away. I immediately connected what I saw in my dream to the Tree of Life presented in Norse and European mythology. But my greatest realisation came from contemplating my vision after.

It came to me that we are the fruit of the Tree of Life (or Light) in a very direct sense of this expression. Our evolutionary history doesn't begin in the human realm. You started as trees or plants, which The Tree of Life had sewn the seeds of. Then we became insects and beasts only to become human later. For me the difference became apparent in memory.

I had another vision where a single seed of a prehistoric dandelion tree (not flower) was blown by the wind. As it is being blown by the wind and descends, it develops limbs and becomes a sort of stick insect upon landing. This was for me a profound and humbling experience. For the first time I had started to understand nature and life in a full and meaningful way. It seemed that all the pieces of the puzzle had come together. I saw the most important moon flower there is. One of the many ways in which my life had begun. A way to understand natural history through submitting to size is nothing. The divinity of my nature is something *I realised fully. Cosmic egg. You were created as small insects first and then through conversations with the Tree of Light via dreams and long aware thought understood what to seek and when to seek it. Everyone has their journey. The dandelion tree was what gave us life and form. The rest was a gift.*

Throughout our cosmic evolution, the Tree of Life sends us dreams and evaluates whether the state of our soul is fit for life in human form. We still undergo this process because our actions are tied to us through Karma. It is an evolution of sorts.

The Divine Trees produce a variety of 'life seeds'. Moon, star and planetary seeds are just examples of a few. All these are different and are given the opportunity to manifest their soul in human form. All of these seeds have a unique potency and through them becoming animated beings they develop their individual traits further.

The process of evolution is extremely lengthy. We are only at the beginning of the first phase of the universe. The process of natural selection is at play, however it is manifested through spiritual evolution rather than selection.

Later I discovered that the Tree of Life sews embryos from which other insects appear, butterflies and bees among many others. The human journey is not uniform and our cosmogenesis is individual and independent.

The force which the Tree of Life embodies maintains the process of spontaneous generation. This is an organic process in the realm of human understanding. This process is the birth of the soul and occurs in the lights of both the male and female trees. This is further supported by the principle of cause and effect.

I had learnt that in my early life form I was a prehistoric bee species which grew to about the size of a bird and had humanoid, monkey-like facial features.

The consumed pollen which had a psychoactive effect shaped the resonance and calendar of the souls birthing process. I even remember that upon ingesting the pollen the colour of the sky was changing. It was a truly beautiful memory where I felt I was a part of something great, transcendent and whole.

I saw nature as a complete system of life force for the very first time. The Tree of Life is the source of many life forms, humans, insects and plants, however there are other Great Trees which exist.

They are described as angels in Christianity and Judaism and when people describe speaking to entities they are describing a conversation with either The Tree of Light or one of the other Trees of Cosmogenesis.

Every Great Tree has an element of the human spirit embodied in itself and emanates all the laws of cosmogenesis in their own unique way. They are incredibly important to our personal development. One can meditate and converse with them through dreams. They appear in human and animal forms when one is asleep.

Both the Tree of Life and The Trees of Cosmogenesis are a divine reflection of human consciousness. The Tree of Life is the maternal and paternal force (there are ofcourse male and female trees).

The Trees of Cosmogenesis, like the Trees of Light, are capable of connecting to our psyche. This process is that which makes our dreams and as a result, our psyche reflects in the collective consciousness of the whole and is constantly reflecting with the divine purpose. This is done through the pollen in the air we breathe and not only.

They are trees as well as smaller plants like Datura. These plants are conscious bodies which evaluate the state of mind and spirit that one finds themselves in and permeate universal law and order within the living biome. They are what judge our being and decide upon destiny. Datura works and tries to understand how a person is experiencing life in deeper aspects relating to the world that surrounds them. It is a sacred plant and must be treated with respect. I do not support the use of Datura to induce a psychedelic experience.

When we experience a fantastic dream, it is often these plants that are responsible for it. They are the source of cryptic and prophetic thought like that of the Oracle of Delfi.

There is not just one Tree of Life, but many thousands. Each Tree is responsible for creating men and women and keeping the human world in balance. This diversity is pictured in religions around the world in the form of different deities and cults. The Trees are responsible for the creation of our universe and the solar system.

As mentioned in the previous chapter, space is very big. We do not live in the same dimension of space as The Tree, not to say that it is superficial. The space itself is a structure which upholds the law of order. Space has different characteristics and different laws of nature are upheld because of its property. Every universe bubble has conditions fine tuned to a specific experience and purpose. This particular world is created by the Tree of Light and natural laws operate within the mean of nature's definition as well as the worlds. It is the world which is resonant and the fact that it is created does not exclude it from the world law of order.

Upon discovering the source of existence many things fell into place. I realised Akasha, understood astrology and life after death became a certainty for me. Many religious principles became apparent and I began to sense a feeling of wholeness within.

My realisation came at a very difficult time for me, and seeing this Tree in a wakeful state to this day is the greatest epiphany I have had. I felt a profound sense of peace and purpose. Seeing this magnificent being, and knowing that it is what gave me life was humbling and many beautiful emotions were evoked within me. I felt a comforting feeling that there was a reason for all of my experiences and that life was no accident.

We connect to the Trees which gave us life through spirit during our sleep every evening. The Trees are all knowing and give everyone the opportunity they deserve. With life comes responsibility and through my discovery I deem it appropriate to share this message with as many people as possible. It is something which I believe was lost because of religious conflict and ignorance. We are the children of these great Trees.

The Tree of Light is what holds our soul at the moment of death. It is what gives us life afterwards. Everything is relative and resonant from the principle of objectivity. The Tree is a very delicate structure despite its mighty appearance. The purity of our souls must be maintained for the Tree to be healthy and eternal.

Survival of the Fittest

The Darwinian concept of natural selection is something I have come to accept as a part of the divine. We are all a personification of the cosmos and a different aspect of it, and therefore, it is up to us to evolve physically and spiritually through the time we are given.

It is up to the individual to resonate with the human essence in the most beautiful way. This is manifested by people today through the search for a calling or an attempt of fulfilling individual desires which take the form of artistic or scientific work as well as undertakings in a beautiful romantic life.

The beginning of higher consciousness manifesting in an individual is the seeking of their own mission and place in the world. It is a quality which does not manifest in every individual. The individual who experiences such a need of purpose, sometimes sees it as a burden, however it is something that should be embraced and nurtured by everyone.

Through my access to the Akashic records I found a discussion pertaining to the great plan for humanity. Unfortunately not all of us will meet in what the bible described as heaven, however it was made clear to me that one must be a well rounded soul and exhibit the inclination to learn and explore the truth, which in itself is a form of enlightenment.

The Tree of Life decides where and when we are to live. It can also banish individuals from life altogether if a serious sin is committed, the individual doesn't progress spiritually or stops resonating with the core human principles.

It is therefore important for one to live a good life in accord with classical morality. One should also make it a priority to have an individual spirituality and practice mindfulness and personal development. In today's age it is a challenge but every one of us has been put here for a reason.

I was told that for me to develop my being further I must strengthen and practise vital life energies. These energies are an aid in maintaining awareness at death and help with individual omnipotence. We should all strive towards greatness. Life is very long and potentially eternal and taking time to meditate upon our own personal 'big picture' is something I would encourage everybody to do.

In certain theories pertaining to angels, it is said that these higher beings have already accomplished degrees in spiritual awakening and development. They are ahead of humans in the evolutionary mission. As a soul which is very old, I have already gone through some of the cycles of spiritual evolution and despite reaching the sphere of immortality I am motivated to evolve further into an elder and then a sage.

I feel slightly bewildered due to the nature of the world I am experiencing. I have never lived in such a developed society and by contrast have spent most of my life nude and under the light of the Sun and stars. I still find it troubling, however the Tree of Light has reassured me that there is a purpose in its actions and in my existence on this planet. I have all the resources to understand how my spirit and body work. I am here to achieve my individual goals.

The initiatory levels of life of the immortal, elder and sage are defined by the individual's way of thinking and spiritual accomplishments. In the highest order, the ability to remember past incarnations is second nature, there is an increase in the awareness of truth and the individual constantly meditates upon the Akashic records and listens to instruction given by the Tree of Life. With this enlightenment comes a field of responsibility and it is the guidance of people and souls through their present incarnation and teaching them the wisdom of life and the Tree of Light.

We are currently in the very first phase of life and the universe. It is the phase of creation. Everyday, individuals are being selected for future life by the Trees of Light and new individuals are being born into the world. The phase of creation began with primordial cosmogenous beasts formed many millions of years ago. These were 'hybrid' beings of enormous size, often dinosaur-like. They are described in many mythologies around the world.

Through this phase it is important to focus on individuation and to focus on creating a unique life experience for one's being. Nature will do its best to take care of people who are actively learning and improving their lives. It is important to live in accordance with moral values and embrace new experiences. Destiny is a concept few will learn to experience. We will each learn our purpose with future incarnations.

It is in this world where we learn and form our true meaning of purpose. This is because purpose is an intrinsic quality of all the functions of the world. Every reflection of divine geometry has the intrinsic quality of purpose and as well as forming the world it is individual. This is a universal principle.

The Akashic Records

The concept of the Akashic records is that it is a compendium of events, thoughts and processes that have and will occur in the ether. Theosophists have argued that it is embedded into space itself. In actuality it is knowledge given to us by the ever wise Trees of Life and Trees of Cosmogenesis.

Each of us has a chapter within these records. One can access memories from previous incarnations. I have been privileged to access my own records in the form of memories. I have very vivid visions of my own being in other life forms as well as specific events which happened in the primordial phases of my existence. I also have insight into certain events pertaining to the 'general evolution' of life that had happened throughout time.

It came to me that a certain species of wasp was capable of influencing the growth and characteristics of plants with the venom released by their stinger. There was an event, where a few wasps were absorbed by tree resin. This phenomenon is seen on this planet as fossilised wasps appearing in the mineral of amber. The tree digested, processed and evolved within its system. By cross pollination other trees evolved alongside it. There is a Great Tree whose fruit as a result of this process is a bird, yes, a bird! The universe where this had happened was created by the Tree of Light and was not an entirely 'wild' example of space.

In connection to the absorption of the insect, we see the formation of plants such as orchids and the Venus Fly Trap. As stated above, these trees evolved. There was a tree which attracted wasps into its flower and the shape of the flower was like that of the Venus Fly Trap.

The wasps flew into the flower and split open the membrane to taste the sap. As the derivative of this sap was from the death of an ancestor, the sap itself was psychedelic. The wasps fell asleep and became aware of their dream state. Some of the bees overdosed and passed however the nature of the psychedelic sap was able to wake them up from their death. They were also aroused and started to fly into the flower in pairs and began to enjoy intercourse in this psychoactive state.

This event was no accident. The collective of the Great Trees was trying to study the mechanics of dreaming, life after death and anatomy. It is also a gift bestowed upon certain individuals at that early phase of their existence and is still expressed for them today.

The Trees did this, because they knew that the most profound fruit they could create was human. Like every organism, there is intrinsic knowledge that is held by the Great Trees. They know how they function in the world.

The definite purpose of this event is still unknown to me, although I believe it is rooted in the alchemical evolution of man and consciousness.

Without the concept of The Tree of Life being at the core of our existence, the Akashic records seem like a very leftfield theory which has little to no scientific grounding.

When we apply the knowledge of the Tree of Life to the world and our daily life and make it the forefront of our contemplation, we can substantiate a full, coherent and organic worldview, which takes into account everything that is bound by nature. This state of consciousness has transformed my life in a profound way. I am able to understand very complex dreams, karma, life after death and my evolutionary history.

The Tree of Life is the being which people have come to describe as God. Any spiritual experience can be attributed to the Tree of Life. Everything happens for a reason. Even you reading this work is a sign that you are looking for truth and a sign that you're heading towards the emanation of light from this universal truth.

The Divine Within

Everyone of us has an element of the divine within themselves. The Divine Tree of Life gave a piece of its wonder to us and this is for us to develop individually. This gift manifests itself through the love we give to one another and also through our own ability to develop a uniquely functioning organism.

It is in the arts of alchemy and magic where one studies and begins to practise an acquaintance with the gifts bestowed upon him or her. The magnificence of the gifts are dependent on the karmic balance accumulated throughout the souls lifetime, thus action is one of the most important things in an individual's journey. It is imperative to keep this at the forefront of one's mind when living day to day. Becoming stagnant is one of my greatest frustrations. I always aim to push my spiritual development as far and without rest.

One must think of ways to improve in the most important fields of life. It is pointless doing the same meditation over and over. After reaching a plateau one must find a way to elevate the practice to achieve greater things. It is the exact same in all aspects of life, however application in the most important arts are of magnificent reward.

When pursuing alchemical transformation it is important to note that only general principles can be placed in a handbook. The process of development is highly individual and cannot be quantified via objective and general study. One must discover their own path of light.

Biological individuation is something we will be able to achieve in future incarnations. It is already an achievement on the level of the individual. We will be able to form our own archetypes and live alongside people who are truly individuals. Within my body this process has already begun. I have experienced many transformations of the mind and physical body as well as visions regarding the various biophysical models of our body.

There are archetypes upon archetypes. It is a virtual infinity. People will form their own ideas of the human body and express them alongside others. There will be different archetypes living alongside one another and they will display biophysical individuation. This is not only in application of the human energy body but also in the art of sexual magic.

In the future, the sexual process will become a psychedelic experience and besides reproduction, we will be able to enjoy sex for its pleasure. We will separate reproductive functions and be able to decide when to give life. Sexual magic is the most powerful form of magic there is. Our bodies are not yet developed in a way where we can practise the metaphysical aspects of this art. We can only experience the physical nature of sex.

There exists a structure within our body which is like that of the branches of a tree. It is not evolved in our body and exists only as a seed, waiting for its conception. It is a seed from the Tree of Life which we keep within us.

I have experienced a feeling of this structure manifesting. I saw a hologram of a body with two branches growing inside the chest. A few nights later I experienced this form being conceived within my body. I had felt it as if it had appeared overnight. The structure has oval shaped fruits hanging from each of the two branches around the area of the pectorals. These can hold the force and essence of flowers, fruits and nuts and are used in the practice of sexual magic. They will be what makes our fruits of love psychedelic and potent.

Within the structure of the tree, lies a source of divine energy which emanates from the Tree of Light. One can meditate upon different divine trees like the Baobab or Oak and input the divine frequencies and even mix different plants to form a unique source. Once again we see an example of divine natural alchemy at work. It is one of the highest levels of understanding of Green Magic.

In this life, I have experienced the psychedelic nature of the sexual act through euphoria, aural and visual hallucinations directly after intercourse. I stress that the act of sexuality is very powerful. It is important who we decide to enjoy our fruit with. Neglecting one's self in this aspect can lead to a deep psychological trauma.

To give life is undoubtedly one of the most divine aspects of woman. During every lunar cycle the woman connects to the spirit of The Tree of Life and is given a soul's dream to bear within her being. The consciousness of new life lies within the female form. My mother has told me that I used to appear in her dreams before I was born. We already connected through spirit.

When a child is in the womb it converses with the mother. There is an eternal connection between the two individuals. In my past incarnations I remember that children used to show symbols to their mother when she was in pregnancy. Those were universal symbols all people understood. They became part of culture and were the subject of stories and myth.

It is important to note that all spiritual gifts have their source in the Tree of Light. Without its watchful eye, the individual is only able to achieve deep contemplation, and even this is of credit to the Tree.

Our intellect is a divine energy which we must cultivate and collect judgments and knowledge of. It is important to occupy one's mind with thinking which is full and of great meaning. When this is done, we stimulate our vital energy force and make it more attune to the ideal we are trying to achieve. Our first gift is that of beauty and our second is that of intellect. We must unite these two concepts in the realm of thought to open doors to higher understanding and the higher modes of consciousness.

The Tree of Light has led me to a beautiful place, where I am living consciously in the best way that is currently possible. It is important for us to seek its divine light openly and with beautiful intention. I encourage everyone to ask for things that are of importance to the spirit. It can be as little as asking for a dream. Manifestation of physical things is also attainable although this practice requires humility and is something most of us can individually achieve.

One can ask each night before going to sleep for a dream or conversation. I suggest making it a daily practice for those who are just beginning their spiritual path of awakening and are dedicated and sincere. The Holy Trees will respond and even though it is possible you will not be able to recall the experience, know that The Trees have listened. Look for spirits in the forms of humans, animals, plants or rivers when dreaming. If control of the dream is gained, try to focus and understand what you are doing there. Converse with these spirits and ask meaningful questions.

Men and women have glands within the mind which enable us to connect with the divine source of the Trees of Life. These are often associated with the power of the Third Eye. This inner vision must be something we make the most of. One can access the power of the inner vision without opening the Third Eye. The analysis of dreams, coupled with meditation are the first steps one must take to access the power of this inner vision.

Chapter Three: The Energy Body

The Hermetic Principles

The study of Hermeticism is that of higher faculty. It focuses on the aspects of astrology, philosophy, religious practice, alchemy and the study of the manipulation of energy. I believe that knowledge of the possibility of manipulating energy was second nature amongst Hermetic scholars of the ancient age.

Hermetic philosophy should be applied to everyday life. The precepts are universal and aim to structure an understanding of the world based upon a system of internal mechanism and reflection. It places the student at the centre of the philosophy and allows for personal development as well as the development of spirit.

There are seven keys of understanding within Hermetic philosophy known as the seven Hermetic principles. Each Hermetic principle has a grounding within the science of physics and has a metaphysical reflection within human manifestation of form, intellect and world ideal. The principles aim to show the adept a key to reason and study, as well as the understanding of the biological systems of energy manipulation.

It is wise to apply the principles to meditation, philosophy and practical work regarding energy manifestation. The principles are a philosophy in themselves.

The first principle is the principle of mentalism. It states that "all is mind". It aims to highlight the power that perception and knowledge have upon consciousness and the process of inquiry, as well as to underlie that the power to manipulate energy lies within the mind. It is said that 'beauty is in the eye of the beholder'. We can interpret this saying through this principle, where the object or knowledge which is sought will be at the forefront of our inquiry and it will be that which will inevitably be found. When applying this principle to meditation we see that intention is what is highlighted here. Our focus must be one of intention.

The principle of correspondence, or, as above, so below, is a general philosophical principle of symmetry between the macrocosm and the microcosm. Respecting the will of the divine, everything manifests in symmetrical and relatable structures. We see this principle in all aspects of science. This principle is to be applied to a meditation exercise when one has awakened Kundalini and is practising the actual art of manifesting energy, placing equal temperament on generating and expressing the force. It describes an underlying principle of relativity amongst all things, phenomena, thoughts and energies. It is also a stress on health. What is input is transformed and through the principle of correspondence an adequate result is the outcome.

The principle of vibration states that everything is in a constant motion, or flux. It is a principle which describes the animate nature of the void as well as energy manifestations. It can be applied to various meditation exercises which relate to breathing work and focus meditations. It teaches us that vibration is something malleable and something we can influence as human beings. It is imperative to know how an object vibrates or functions before attempting any energy work upon it.

The principle of polarity teaches us the law of opposing forces. A simple example is that of light and darkness or that of male and female. It is a focus on the complementation of opposites. Even the principle of divinity, God or the monad has a complimentary force that is human nature. In energy manipulation this principle shows the nature of energy and the relationship energy has with the targeted field. It is cold so it must become hot and vice versa. This is a practical knowledge where the student can develop concepts of energy that are to be used on different media and in different disciplines.

The principle of rhythm is quite obscure. It is similar to the law of vibration and polarity. Its direct implication in energy manipulation is that of understanding the various phases of energy which are manifested. It is also a principle relating to the natural clock of the world, body and the entire energy system of the world. There is a time where energy is accumulated and when energy is released. This natural rhythm is something the student must keep in balance.

The principle of gender states that gender manifests on all planes of existence. It is true. There exist positively charged protons and negatively charged electrons. There is matter which can store an energetic charge. It is similar to the principle of correspondence. It shows unity within all macrocosmic, and microcosmic natural systems and even the created ones. In energy manipulation it shows that certain energies are applied to specific fields and need to be tailored to the nature of work and the object in question.

Knowledge of the seven principles are to be applied to the energy body, philosophy and daily life. Contemplation and application in day to day existence and personal philosophy is essential to undertake the process of activating and understanding the systems withheld in the energy body. One must apply these ideas in meditation and study to grasp the whole nature of their inquiry. To understand a thing fully is to understand everything about it, even its opposites. They are essential in understanding truth. The principles are manifestations of higher consciousness modality.

The Four Grand Structures of the Energy Body

Through deep meditation I have managed to observe four great structures which constitute the energy body. When focusing on specific energies I began to perceive holographic images which appeared as individually different yet connected systems. These four systems are The Qabbalistic Sefira, The Caduceus System, The Three Nadis & The Kundalini. These three systems are all interconnected and form a web of pathways which carry and transmute energy.

These systems have been the focus of study of many groups such as the The Masonic and Rosicrucian orders of the modern era as well as nearly all of the ancient schools of wisdom. Their meditations focus on enhancing and developing the energy body in a way which will enable the individual to experience its formation consciously.

The Quabbalistic Sefira, The Caduceus, The Three Nadis & The Kundalini are a manifestation of the energy body which in peak evolutionary conditions allows for the individual to manipulate and generate energy omnipotently within the body and on the exterior. They are also what constitute alchemical transformation.

Because of the nature of the world we live in, we are unable, at this current moment, to go beyond the law of manifestation and attraction to any significant degree. The alchemical transformation happens on a subtle level and may go unnoticed. Those who have awakened any one of those systems are at the beginning of their evolutionary journey which will enable them to manifest energy at will and apply it to their daily life and for the benefit of others. These energies can be applied to fields like medicine, herbalism, fire making, rock shaping & water work.

In the future, our world will be like that of a playground, where humans will be able to create a world of their own. This will involve things like advanced agriculture, the finding and developing of advanced water systems and other essential things. These fields of study exist today in a very basic form. The systems I am describing are highly advanced and some examples of progress may be seen in pre-Columbian Americas. Their developments of the Nazca lines, irrigation systems and Terra Preta were all incredible achievements for their time. There will be a time when humans will be able to develop specific water types and tools of all sorts with the use of energy and precious minerals.

The system of the Three Nadis is a system that distributes and generates energy, in fantasy this energy is known as 'mana'. Mana has elemental characteristics and although each individual develops every element, the archetypal nature of man and the universe means that there is a dominant elemental energy present throughout the system. There are many types of energy, mainly water, earth, fire, air and aether. The simplest way to describe their diversity is through the use of celestial fields. The main ones that come to mind are star, planetary & lunar types, although there are also ways to implement precious minerals into the field we are trying to generate. There can be planetary or lunar water for example.

The way of describing energy via the elements is merely a representation. It is more accurate to implement the use of precious minerals to describe it. One can of course spawn fire but it is only a characteristic of the force, and not the direct quality of the energy used to manifest the force.

In the system of the Three Nadis it is the aer which is the force of manifesting. It is a celestial energy which has to be practised by the individual to achieve mastery over the elements, energy and one's own body. When looking at this system through the lens of physics the system's property is that which constitutes life's vitality. It is the force which upholds the structure of manifested energy and allows for it to have an effect. This manifested energy is the vital life force.

This system is the flow of vital energies which is distributed to the organs of the individual. The energy flowing through it can be of different quality, tailored to the individual's desire. The potential of this energy is extremely high.

In higher states of evolution this system is developed further, to a system which allows for the manipulation of energy. This force has all the elements enclosed in it and is what allows for energy to visibly manifest.

The archetypal nature of man means that every one of us will be able to focus on a specific aspect of our energy force and manifest it to its fullest potential.

The Kundalini is a system of energies which corresponds to the organs as well as our energy body. It is a system which is essential to the alchemical and spiritual development of our beings. It is responsible for our growth when reaching maturity as well as maintaining a healthy balance and tension of energy within our bodies which is responsible for our wellbeing.

Each chakra within the kundalini is an individual sacred geometric structure. The stellated platonic solids are a good starting point in one's study. In a mathematical sense these shapes are only representations of a general principle and in reality are a lot more complex.

Each chakra is a modal restructuring of the Flower of Life. The Flower of Life itself represents the manifested energy and has been a key of study of many ancient civilizations. It withholds mathematical models of ratio as well as information regarding the formation of the eye, our bodies and the bodies of all life forms, our consciousness and the formation of the world.

The Chakras are what form the mineral points in all the organs and glands of our bodies and distribute energy to those points which heightens or lowers the intensity that the organs operate in.

The energy of The Caduceus system possesses the soul's imprint. Each energy decision we make carries a consequence and also carries our individual soul energy. It carries our angelic name as well as a bio-energetic watermark.

After the conception of this energy I saw a holographic image of two white snakes ascending a staff. In classical alchemy the snakes represent the opposing forces of water and fire or the Moon and the Sun. The two snakes show the polarity of energy and life force and in psychology represent the duality of male and female. It is the pure vital force.

This system is connected to both the Kundalini and the Three Nadis. The system is a whole and not something to be looked at separately. Serpent imagery is something which occurs in the cultural aspect of Kundalini. The Buddhas and Yogis are often presented with serpents. The nature of Kundalini is energetic and the staff depicts a system which is adjacent to it.

The use of the symbol in the fields of medicine shows its true nature. The serpents and staff are a healing force. The whole symbol comprises four elements which are four different energies.

The staff is the force of will and order. It is associated with wisdom and decision making. It is the energy which is capable of manifesting desired frequencies in the chakras as well as the mineral points of the organs or other energy fields.

The snakes are a system of energy which represent water and fire. The myth of the fruit being eaten from the Tree of Knowledge of Good and Evil is a parable of the power which one holds when the kundalini system is active. Its proper use is that of maintenance and purity. The Tree holds both the knowledge of Good and the knowledge of Evil. It is bipolar. In the application of medicine the forces are that can ignite or extinguish desired energies within the body.

The wings in the whole symbol represent aer. They are the energies which can heal illness that is of deeper nature and potentially threatening to future lives.

In iconography and fantasy, the staff is often decorated with a precious mineral. That is why the whole system has four rather than three elements of character. The precious gem is the symbol of higher evolution and the application of this system to the art of energy manipulation.

The Caduceus system is deeply connected to our soul and development of the mind and has many archetypes. It is apparent that in many mythologies there is a sacred totemic object which is a representation and archetype of the Caduceus. For instance we see it as King Arthur's sword.

The geometric structure of the Qabalistic Tree of Life is a representation of the modality of energy. The sefiroth are organised in a geometric structure and through the combination or subtraction of sefira one can achieve different modes of energy. There are many of these modes and a detailed study of the Qabalah is essential for its understanding and implementation. The Sefira, organised in different aspects, are the manifested symbol of various energetic principles. These principles are of elemental nature. One can produce elemental energies and the mineral qualities of such elements within a summoned energy.

In essence, the Qabala is a map and model of energy which has many applications. In the context of the Kundalini it demonstrates energy phases and structures relating to the operation of organs and bodily functions. In higher forms of being, it also holds the keys to energy manipulation.

Qabalah is not only applied to the study of energy manifestation but to the general auric field of our bodies. Despite the assignment of planets to each sefiroth as a base model, this celestial assignment can be changed by the individual and through the proper use of the Kundalini and Caduceus energy systems one can begin to heal our bodies and further practise energy manipulation which have both the applications in medicine as well as in the more physical nature of the craft.

It seems that the Kundalini system is associated with deep spiritual practices despite its nature being in the field of medicine. It is because it enables the mind to develop higher energies which allow the individual to experience higher states of consciousness. Once functioning correctly we can begin to experience memories of past incarnations as well as accessing higher knowledge and wisdom.

Kundalini & The Cosmic Self

My spiritual journey started in the year 2017. My first experience was a dynamic swoosh of energy that I felt in the thalamic region of the brain, known in Eastern thought as the 'Cave of Brahma'. In new age thinking it is described as the Third Eye. This swoosh had a very specific energetic force which my intuition attributed to the planet Neptune. Without going into detail, it felt like a Neptunian force and nothing else could describe it in a better way.

When studying archetypes in mythology, one can reach the conclusion that the matter of each individual mind is attached to a specific planetary field. Many of the Gods in ancient religions around the world are a manifestation of the collective unconscious and the phenomenon of Kundalini.

Kundalini is a group of energy centres and pathways of a human's energy system. These energies are connected to the stars and planets. The energy is archetypal and is different in everyone. Kundalini awakening can lead to a deeper connection with the universe, experiencing conversations with The Divine Source, memory of past lives, and at the highest level: development and transformation of anatomy, not just in the mind but also the body.

Kundalini energy can be divided into 'static' and 'motive' energy. The static fields such as root or third eye chakra are connected to our magnetic field and our organs. Motive energy is an energy which can travel in longitude of the chakras. It grows in magnitude and has the potential to develop the static fields.

Many of you have heard the term Solar Plexus. We have more than one type of plexi at our disposal. Some beings have a Solar Plexus while others have a Lunar or Planetary plexus. This chakra, like all the others, is made up of at least three polarities of energy: planetary, lunar and star energies. These polarities have different geometric combinations based on the geometry of the flower of life. Through meditation one can activate and mould these energies individually in the waking state. In most people these transformations happen during sleep.

Our feelings and awareness are often overridden by neglecting the energy that is stored in the Kundalini system. Through unawareness of our being we develop our personalities and traits which are influenced by the energies emanating from the Kundalini.

This state is a subtle psychosis and is experienced by most people. It is imperative that we analyse our speech and thinking to fully understand this. Sometimes we say things out of laziness or spite. These are manifestations of this subtle psychosis. When one reaches a transcendent state, arguments become a futile and agonising activity.

The phenomenon of Kundalini has been depicted by many religions around the world and in the form of mythology. In the Indian subcontinent, it has been known for thousands of years and is deeply embedded in the culture of those people. In western culture it has been symbolised and taught through the form of myth.

A good example is Greek or Roman mythology. The forms of the Gods represent an organised model of activated kundalini. This is a phenomenon which stems most likely from unawareness and is manifested by the phenomenon of the collective unconscious as discovered by Carl Jung.

In modern pop culture/alternative history/conspiracy theories, we often hear of people coming from different constellations, ie. Pleiades or Sirius. This is the same phenomenon also linked to a specific field of the Kundalini force which we can discover using our intuition. Those speculations are also manifestations of the subtle psychosis described earlier.

My Kundalini journey has been filled with turmoil and at the same time immense beauty. After ingesting psilocybin mushrooms, I had stimulated my kundalini like never before during meditation. It was a shock to my system. I experienced wave after wave of paranoia and at times, I felt like I was speaking to a demon. This wave of psychosis subsided with the opening of my Third Eye. I was seeing everything in a new light, and was and still am incredibly grateful that I have been able to experience this in a waking state. Little I had known, this was only the beginning.

Chapter Four: Experience & Meditation

Lotus Energies & Sacred Geometry

We each hold within us the aspect of our divine Tree of Light. It is manifested in our bodies and is known to the Eastern schools as Kundalini and through the symbol of the lotus flower.

The symbols of the lotus and mandala are closely linked to Kundalini. In the years of 2017-2020 I witnessed the formation of the Lotus energies and the Lotus itself. It all began with the opening of my Third Eye in 2017. In the morning I had woken up and instantly felt a swoosh in the membrane of my Thalamic Region. In the east it is known as the Cave of Brahma. The word Thalami in Greek means chamber or chambers. In the yogic schools, it is the region where the Third Eye chakra is located known as Ajna or the Bindu. In many yogic practices it is stressed that one should focus on that region and there, the practitioner will feel one with the divine and emanate its light within.

It was the beginning of one of the most mystical processes I have experienced. A few months later, I had felt two glorious energies manifest in my mind. I had felt the energies of Jupiter and Saturn manifest in a brilliant bright and expressive energy. I wonder to this day what this means for my life. It cannot be an accident. A few months later the same thing happened, this time with the planet Uranus and later the planet Neptune. All the energies were distinct and the only thing that could describe their characteristic were the gaseous planets. It was truly spectacular.

In total, I have felt 7 spheres of this type of energy. There was one further force of the moon Ariel, which had appeared as if it was connecting the four planetary centres. It appeared in the frontal lobe, then jumped from Jupiter to Saturn and then from Uranus to Neptune.

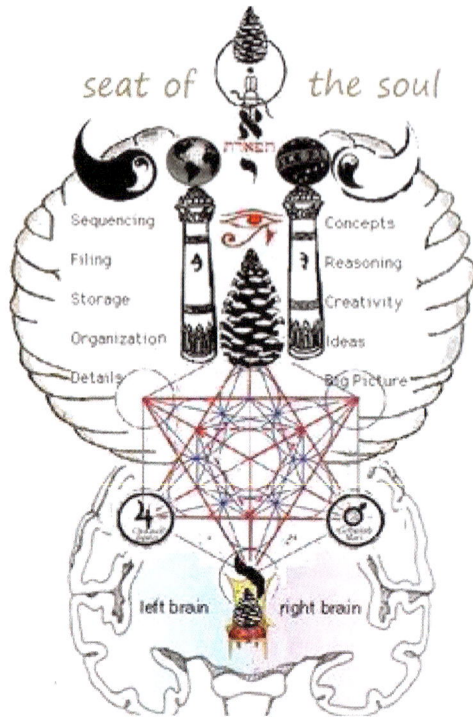

seat of the soul

I had wondered whether I lost my mind, however with research I managed to find a diagram which depicted what I had experienced, which was reassuring. We see the Eye of Chorus which represents the Third Eye, the spheres which represent the location of the planetary energies and the pinecone which represents a sacred structure within the brain itself. It is what releases the mythical substance of ambrosia in one's system.

About two weeks after the four planetary energies had manifested I had felt something truly spectacular. A jelly substance started to grow above my thalamus and proceeded to grow all over my brain. Its shape was like a spiky ball which grew its spikes throughout my system. It continued to grow for a couple of days and then it grew throughout my whole body. In the mind, its geometry became profound. It displayed beautiful floral geometry. It had rings around it which moved up and down along its main stem. It was incredible.

This 'flower of the mind' is something unique in every individual. There are many different substances which can generate this unique form. The structure is dependent on what planetary energy manifests within our mind's subtle body. It is an element of the divine Tree of Life that we hold within our bodies.

As divine beings, we are connected to the energy of the planets. All of our minds have different 'ruling planets', not in the astrological sense, but in the metaphysical and physiological aspects. It is the energy field that our mind operates in as well as the field which makes up our brain matter. This is the energy which manifests an archetype within our body and is also the archetypal force of our soul.

This awakening is a gift from The Tree of Life. During my awakening I was told a story of a young boy who had this happen to him during a wakeful state. It is said that the people of that world thought he was ill and decided that he should live in seclusion. People brought him food, however he was ostracised and forced to live his life away from his people. I am grateful that I was able to experience this in a safe place and that I am able to share this experience with people without being judged as ill.

Months had passed and I continued to wonder upon how my mind had changed. To this day, I do not fully understand what had happened. Meditation yielded comfort but no coherent answers were found. While studying Sacred Geometry I came to the realisation that we can apply it to our minds' chemistry and discover chemicals which reflect different aspects of the Flower of Life.

I started to explore the relationship between spirit animals and the mind geometry. The Buddha and also Shiva are often presented with serpents and birds surrounding them. The image of a tree is often focal.

I am not sure whether this was through a dream or meditation but I had realised that there was a substrate of the mind which corresponded to spirit animals. It is a chemical form. I started to meditate upon this and chose animals and birds that represented what I found most fascinating. I had selected bees, hummingbirds, the salamander, the dragonfly, the butterfly and others. The brain is geometrically and chemically constructed in a way where divine proportion reflects itself within its physical and chemical structure.

Each time I meditated upon a specific animal, an area of the brain would 'light up' and activate with a corresponding shape and structure. For instance the bee was located in the Cerebellum whereas the hummingbird's beak felt like it was pouring a liquid into the newly formed floral structure. I had chosen these animals because of their relation to honey. I saw honey as a one of nature's wonders and because of the psychedelic honey which is present in Nepal, I see that it has many more spiritual mysteries which it encompasses within itself as a symbol.

This experience yielded an alchemical transformation which occurred within the substrate of my mind. I had felt as if the whole of my mind turned into a gas and was replaced by crystal formations. This of course was a biochemical illusion. The structure was complex. I had felt the formation of bee wings within the empty space. I could perceive all the shapes and the makeup of the crystals and wings. The wings are symbolised in culture as the Petasos of the Greek God Hermes. There are many archetypal forms of this phenomenon. I believe it was the evolution of a neurotransmitter and its network.

Greek & Roman mythologies are fantastic examples of the collective unconscious manifesting concepts of divine geometry within the mind. The Gods described in the Pantheon are archetypes of biochemical structures within the mind and those of the Kundalini. Each God is accompanied by a specific cult and symbology attached to worship.

If we take the Greek God of the Sun, Apollo, we see that his symbols are the laurel wreath, lyre, bow and arrow, the Raven, the Swan and the Wolf. Each symbol is a specific property of the archetype which is reflected by the sacred geometry of the mind. The laurel wreath is the most obvious example. It is an item which is worn around the head by royalty. It is the equivalent of the lotus symbol which symbolises the 'flower' described in the 'Lotus Energies' chapter. The other symbols are connected to the workings of the Kundalini and it was a way of metaphor that was taught to students and the elites of those times.

The offspring and consort represent a further variation in archetype, connected to the Lunar, Planetary & Star energies which can manifest within a given archetype. The Raven & Swan would be the equivalent symbol for that of the Hermean petasos.

This analogy of representation can be applied to various religions around the world, and not only. We can find a grain of truth in most structured arguments. The fact that one has conjured an idea is enough to give credit to the intellect held within the unconscious and render truth held within its nature, even if it exemplifies a fallacy.

Our brain and soul are connected to The Tree of Light in a way of spirit. It is why certain energies can manifest within the mind. It does not happen spontaneously and without the intent of The Tree of Light. Once a gift is received the greatest way to show appreciation is through progress and meditation.

The Tree of Light is the entity which gives an individual their enlightenment. A way of individual mastery is impossible, and many great minds experienced the glory of enlightenment without knowledge of how and why the Tree of Light works. It is imperative we realise that we are its children and stay humble and wait for our turn to accomplish fulfilment.

The Third Eye, The Chakras and The Light Body

The process of opening the Third Eye is largely misunderstood in today's world. It is often associated with just the pineal gland. The process is a lot more complex, and the term should be applied to the whole brain rather than to a small gland like the pineal. In my experience, I felt a shift in my brain tissue located somewhere around the thalamic region. The area of the shift was approximately an inch and a half, an area a lot larger than the pineal gland. Later on in my development I had felt shifts of similar nature in the whole of my brain tissue.

The awakening of the Third Eye is a neurological activation, where dormant synapses and neurons are activated. Through their activation they develop new neural energy as well as sacred brain chemistry, which is a medium for us to meditate and communicate with the Tree of Light.

This chemistry, apart from being a medium, is what enables us to manifest planetary energies which we develop throughout our lives. They are actively stored by those dormant synapses and upon activation, they are released into constructed systems. They are the system of the light body and are a part of the inner alchemical transformation or evolution.

Our light body is a form which is tied and developed using planetary energy and emotive thinking. It is also developed through karmic balance.

Every system in our body has a chakric system attached to it. Whether it is the liver, brain or soul, they all have a schematic of energy which is malleable and can be transformed and developed. Just like the energy body, the light body has chakras. They are not the 7 chakras described in the Eastern Traditions.

The awakening of the Third Eye and the subsequent chemistry which is formed upon its awakening forms many new subtle systems of chakric energy. We undergo the same process of forming the Light Body in every incarnation. When the Third Eye is dormant its operation is not tangible to us. It is in constant connection with the Tree of Light.

The planets which surrounded us in our past lives have been stored within our soul and will be activated once we reach the second phase of cosmic evolution or achieve great things individually. Sometimes this manifestation of planetary energy which I had experienced happened during sleep. The chakras which become activated through Third Eye awakening are still working, their magnitude is of a different nature.

Around the year 2020 I had felt another structure form. It was very peculiar in nature. I experienced a soup of chemicals attributed to the moon Titan which settled in my neural tissue. This developed a series of mineral junctions within the core of my mind. They were spots which started in the brainstem and moved up towards the crown. They were in a vertical line and also in the form of a pyramid.

These mineral points are a part of the Kundalini energy. They are what our heart uses to regulate the phases and intensity of the energy which is provided to our brain. When these are activated one can experience a heightened state of awareness and experience troubles in sleep when not controlled. This is the system of the Crown chakra.

The Light Body which is a chemical formation in the mind is something which is stored in the Akashic field. It comprises all of the information relating to our soul. Apart from holding memories of past incarnations, the Light Body can recall states of energies which we were operating in, from our past lives. Even our early non-human existence is a gift. We all learnt different things and received different gifts.

I have experienced this through the release of energy from the phase of cosmogony, where the planetary energy stored by a cosmogenous beast was released into my brain in the form of chemistry. I could not give a description of the chemical in any celestial body known to me in the solar system. I felt 5 or 6 pulses of a liquid being shot out of the Cave of Brahma. It had a dark quality to it and was lunar. This chemistry settled around the region of the ventricles. Upon its absorption by the area, I could perceive hundreds of tiny spots which seemed like clusters of neurons.

Meditation Practice

I started meditating at around the age of 15. I sat with closed eyes and maintained focus upon my breathing. It was a very simple practice however it is what began my journey of self discovery. Any action aimed towards a better way is a positive one.

As my experiences deepened my understanding and desires for self mastery I have developed a way of meditating with the 7 main chakras that is systematic and quite fun. It requires focus, creativity and patience.

The 7 chakras by default are connected to the planets in a 'base level' sort of way. One can think of it as a 'factory standard'. This factory standard is a gift which we carry from birth. The development of this gift is up to you.

The objective of this meditation is to align and stimulate the chakras very gently, so they begin to resonate. Once this is achieved, their vibration can lead to progress in experiencing Third Eye awakening and other transcendental states. It is quite a fun and creative way of harmonising the chakras.

The first step is to visualise the chakras on your silhouette while meditating. This exercise is there to help you familiarise with how the chakras feel and develop a way of perceiving their resonance all around your body. Our aim is to align the chakras with your awareness. Start by focusing on the Crown. Try to understand what it is and how it affects your feeling, all while maintaining the image of the 7 chakras on your silhouette. Spend as much time as you need on each chakra, systematically working your way down to the Root chakra.

As you move down towards the Root, try to perceive the energy which connects the chakras. This is a very important step. What you will be feeling is the energy flow of the Ida, Pingala and

Sushumna channels. The energy is different in everyone and try to feel how it is flowing in your system.

I would recommend you take your time and do only these two things for the first sessions of your practice. Do this until you feel it is enough and you have a good idea of how each individual chakra feels and can perceive the energy connecting them. I would urge you to have patience.

The second step is very similar although it requires your energy of focus to be manifested within the Sushumna channel. Start with the same things you have done in the first step however this time as well as visualising the 7 chakras on the outline of your body, attempt to visualise a sphere which is your focus energy. This will happen naturally. Start by meditating upon the Crown and work your way down towards the Root taking your time on each chakra. Try not to break this state and when moving from one chakra to the next keep the visualisation of your focus on what is connecting each chakra.

You have now discovered your focus energy. The aim of this exercise is to introduce action to your energy system and familiarise yourself with each field. This practice will improve your self awareness and your goal should be realising how your chakric system is operating and how it feels. Take your time and be patient. Once you have become comfortable with activating your focus energy proceed to the next step.

The third step is to use your focus energy. Begin at the Crown with the visualisation. Think of the planet connected to the chakra and begin to draw the energy into the Sushumna canal. An aid may be to visualise the circle collapsing to the centre while you are attempting this. Do this for every chakra as you work your way down.

Diligent practice should stimulate your energy and you may begin to experience your chakras in a more direct way.

The fourth and final step is to use your focus energy again, however alongside a creative force. Begin by repeating the first 3 steps and as you are doing so try to conceptualise a feeling of the energy of the Sun in your focus field. After completing the first three rounds of feeling, awareness and action come back to the Crown. This time, use your focus to transform the planetary energy that your chakra is into the energy of the Sun. Take time in every chakra. Do this for every sphere and end your meditation.

Although you may be eager to try a new planet or moon straight away, do not do so initially. Take time and meditate on the system and see if you notice any changes. I would spend at least two weeks with each planet to give time for the force to accumulate in your system.

You can apply the same technique to activate any planet or combination you wish. Once you become apt in meditation, be creative and experiment. Choose your favourite moon or planet. It is a very fun process.

The goal of this meditation system is to harmonise all the chakras with one celestial energy to achieve a union in resonance. You may begin to feel a contrasting force. You now have a reference point of your chakras and the energy travelling in the Ida, Pingala and Sushumna canals as well as an overview of what your system was at 'base level'.

Have fun!

The Mind Flower

The Mind Flower is what I described in an earlier segment of this chapter. I would like to reiterate its importance and develop some further thinking upon the nature of its structure. Every one of us has the capability of activating and creating a Mind Flower. These flowers produce fruits and these fruits develop the mind further.

As the Flower was appearing I had felt the structure grow throughout other organs like the heart and liver. This growth was the formation of the nourishment and cleansing mechanism of its system.

I also felt a structure grow within my testicles, as the Mind Flower appeared, which brings forth the notion that this flower's purpose is rooted in sexual alchemy. It is symbolised by the lotus flower in Eastern mythologies. I believe it is the beginning of the alchemical process that transcends our existence. Its purpose is to connect us with the Tree of Life and share its beauty via sexual union.

The structure of the flower is determined by what planetary energies we manage to manifest in our Third Eye and other areas of the mind. As the energy which opened my Third Eye was Neptune, the Flower is of a Neptunian kind. If your Third Eye opens with the help of a different planetary energy, the Flower will have a different structure.

During its appearance it is where I had my first visual memory of a past incarnation. It was very vivid. Since then, I have revelled in more and more visions of my past lives. I will describe these visions in a later segment.

I believe it is the essence of the soul and releases the mythical substance of ambrosia, which enables a transcendental state, the remembering of past lives as well as the practice of sexual alchemy.

When looking at myths, paintings and statues of the ancient cultures we see many symbols that are attached to the meaning of this Mind Flower. Many figures wear a headdress made out of a specific plant or wear helmets and other items of clothing around their head. It is these symbols which represent an archetypal nature of this Mind Flower and show a diversity of its forms.

The study of religion in a deep sense sheds light on the greater principle of the world. There are many fields of study which exemplify the way The Tree of Light has developed systems for man to experience life in a full way. It is important to be grateful and cherish any state which moves us closer to enlightenment.

The power of Kundalini is of dual nature. Apart from medicinal applications it is also a manifestation of energetic states which other people become influenced by. It is important to not abuse this as it will have consequences upon your own life. Be honest and humble.

The Transformation of the Soul

The dimension we are in as Soul beings is the lowest one. This is apparent by the way we have developed the world around us. Greed, adultery, racism and war are all things which have manifested because of anger and our conflict with the divine source. We are easily susceptible to these mechanisms and through our subconscious awareness of superior forms we have become at war with each other.

The Soul is something which is universal and individual at the same time. It is an object which can undergo metamorphosis and parts of it remain eternal through the process of metempsychosis.

There are terms in our spoken language that describe its workings and ideals and this for me is enough to prove that it is something tangible.

Our soul structure is what defines our physiological makeup. Our lifeform is basic. It has the capability to transform, but it does not accommodate any organ which allows for higher functioning, such as the manipulation of energy or an involved sexual alchemy.

Like anything, the Soul has dimensions. It is something that can transform into various forms with a given set of characteristics. It is an elemental structure and can have an element attached to its core and defining characteristic. There are water, earth, fire and air beings.

These elemental characteristics are only the catalytic character of higher soul structures. These higher structures are celestial, which is further divided into planetary, star and other forces based on planetary geometry, and crystalline souls which are high vibration mechanisms which operate at a high and divine ratio of the fibonacci sequence.

This high ratio of the crystalline soul structure is what gives the ability for the formation of a whole new system of anatomy and functioning. It is the soul of the God being.

I have had a vision of a form which can develop the structure of woods and crystals within the anatomy of the human body. It is a completely different system of life which is the most complex living structure in the universe. It is a form which is capable of energy manipulation, teleportation, sexual alchemy at the highest level and the attainment of eternal enlightenment.

As the universe is very young, the beings who are currently in those divine forms face a set of challenges which are different to those who are in the dimension of the Soul which we are currently experiencing.

The reason I am here is because I have not been alive for a very long time. I have my own test and journey ahead of me, and as do you. As someone who is beginning to experience an awareness of past, present and future, I face many challenges brought upon by today's society. I find it very difficult to find valuable information pertaining to individual alchemy and spiritual development. Religions of this world are focused on salvation and this is understandable, however it is a challenge finding a spiritual movement which places the responsibility and tools directly in the hands of the one who is practising within the school.

The soul also places a barrier on the intellectual capabilities as the biological system of our organism is not very efficient compared to the forms in higher dimensions. It is why there are many ambiguities in the occult teachings, especially in the narrative of metaphor. I believe that with the progress of evolution, this current form will cease to exist in the larger timescale of the universe and life.

An individual who has come to an understanding of the play of sacred geometry and form is someone who is beginning to transcend into a higher dimension of soul and consciousness. The path to liberation from this basic form is long however the individual must remain positive and motivated throughout.

The best way to balance our soul is to maintain mindfulness, ambition, curiosity and an openness to spiritual ideas. It is also important to maintain a healthy imagination which is the fire of cosmic evolution. Without imagination, humanity would still be in the stone age.

One can raise the vibration of this current soul state through meditation and careful personal development. It is a challenging undertaking however very fruitful. One must be prepared to dedicate many lives to this process and give themselves over to the Tree of Light and the law of Karma.

The awakening of the Kundalini is the beginning of the ascension process of this Soul. My spiritual experiences are the subsequent developments of soul and spirit which is preparing for the transformation of the soul from elemental to celestial and then crystalline. I am on this planet to learn as much as I can and take knowledge onto future incarnations.

All souls, be it elemental, celestial or crystalline have levels of development within them as well as archetypes which define the nature of the soul. The levels of development are heightened through spiritual evolution and this applies to all three base levels of soul structures. The archetypal force is the force which will uncover your individual divine purpose so you will be able to contribute to your society and live a full life as a complete individual.

There are many reasons for why we are currently in such a low vibrational state. Because our current form had to evolve on this planet to become human, there are many subtle details at play which go far beyond what I can access in the Akashic record. I know that there is a plan and that many people are here for good reason. Be open to finding that reason individually. Even illness has a greater purpose in the aspect of alchemy. Do not fear.

Spiritual Alchemy

To practise spiritual alchemy, one must realise fundamental truths. If one cannot align their thinking with the existence of The Tree of Light and realise their source of life, or at least acknowledge that there is something at the source of his individuality, the practice will bear little or no fruit at all. The Divine Trees have a way of working with individuals who are open to spiritual evolution. Remember that they take everything into account and are doing what is best for you.

In today's age, many of you will not experience anything supernatural due to the nature of society. It is a process which will break down all formed ideals and make you question every action. Things that we normally would take for granted become a meaningless thing we spend our energy on. It is important not to rush into the practice. Understand that with an awakening come responsibilities which are greater than maintaining a job. Once in a heightened state, you will likely seek to maintain and improve your practice and not worry about everyday responsibilities. They hold you down. You may find yourself losing the motivation to pursue material gains and question every relationship that you have made. This can be very challenging and can have a negative effect on you overall. Be careful.

The first step in undertaking the practice of spiritual alchemy is to realise the Divine Tree of Light and contemplate the nature of your soul. I know that we are the children of the Tree of Light and for some people it may be an idea which is too abstract to grasp. For me, it was something I began seeing as a certainty and because of my visions and the synchronicity of my experiences described earlier I need no further proof. The Tree of Light will notice sincerity in all desires and if they are of the right kind. The most important thing is to realise the existence of the Tree of Light.

Once you have done this, I would begin my practice with an active meditation of asking for a conversation with the Tree which gave birth to you. This conversation may take the form of a dream. Try to meditate before sleep and set an intention to maintain a high level of awareness throughout your sleep. Opening a dream journal may be a good start. This will heighten your creative force and therefore boost vital spiritual energies.

The next step is to begin purification and thorough self analysis. Try to analyse how you are in day to day life as well as the things you see in your dreams. You want to try to strip away the layers of ego which are constructed in an unhealthy way. You may find that some relationships are not what you thought they were and are not formed with the fundamentals of friendships and love. I was very self critical and had a tough time accepting certain things about my nature, however through meditation and the help of The Tree of Light I am in a place where I am constantly materialising progress. I have clean and lucid dreams and often dreams which instruct me upon the workings of my mind and the structures which arose, like the Mind Flower.

Realise the power of the planets and stars. These energies are within you and you must aim to activate them whether it is through Kundalini meditation or other means. The meditation exercise described earlier is enough to get you started. It is important to realise the planetary energies which are gifted to you at birth. Use them for your development and accept the gifts with humility and embrace the nature which gifted you them.

These forces run all throughout your body and play a part in fundamental things like circadian rhythms. Try to discover what is already within you before you start to experiment and modify things within your system. However, change is something that can expose the planets within so find your own path.

Understand individuality and be mindful of others and their experiences. Unfortunately, on my journey, I have met many people who were sceptical of my experiences and looked at me in a way which was very hurtful. I have grown strength within me to ignore their comments and let them be. It is important that you do not impose your practise upon people who are ignorant or simply are too busy and do not take an interest. Focus on your own journey and keep yourself motivated. There are many organisations and circles which discuss spirituality without religious context if that is something that disturbs you. Having people around you may be beneficial, although I would recommend practising individually until you reach a point that you feel others may help you progress. Inputs of third persons can be distracting as well as inspiring.

I found mythology to be an indispensable companion to my journey. The symbolism and incredible stories within myth showed me a new way of looking at my experiences and the world around me. They are an irreplaceable source of information and inspiration. Read them from an alchemical perspective as if they were a hidden key and you shall find a never ending source of inspiration for your alchemical practice. I personally found Greek mythology extremely helpful, especially the myths of the Eleusynian mysteries and the mysteries of Orpheus. One must realise that myths are a manifestation of the collective unconscious and hold many truths within them despite being cryptic in nature. They contain a blueprint which is only accessible with the right perspective and correct analytic method.

Study scripts which evoke inspiration and grasp your attention. It is pointless forcing yourself to read material which is of no interest to you or has messages which are inaccessible. Find your inspiration and path. I found a mix of mythology, green magic, alchemy and paganism to be something full and rich. There are many teachings and many perspectives which all help in personal development. If you are a keen alchemist, study the elements, planetary symbols and alchemical metaphors and lore. Learn botany, as drinking herbal potions can induce dreams and induce states of higher thinking.

Be diligent in your practice. Make time and space for your undertakings. The alchemical process is not something that happens over night and it is something which requires a great amount of effort, despite this, it is something which is incredibly rewarding if pursued for the right reason. Realise that what you do now, has implications in your future incarnations and can help your being immensely. Every positive action you take will outcome sometime within the future of your soul and being. It is a good idea to take a step back and realise the great plan for yourself and humanity as a whole. You can become a part of the great plan, but can only do so through your action. Meditate regularly and upon reaching a milestone, make room for regeneration so further development can ensue.

Printed in Great Britain
by Amazon